SEATTLE SOUNDERS F.C.

BY
MARK STEWART

NORWOOD HOUSE PRESS

Chicago, Illinois

NorwoodHouse Press

P.O. Box 316598 • Chicago, Illinois 60631
For more information about Norwood House Press please visit our website at
www.norwoodhousepress.com or call 866-565-2900.

Photography and Collectibles:
The trading cards and other memorabilia assembled in the background for this book's cover and interior pages
are all part of the author's collection and are reproduced for educational and artistic purposes.

All photos courtesy of Associated Press except the following individual photos and artifacts (page numbers):
Topps, Inc. (6, 10 bottom, 11 top & bottom, 16), The Upper Deck Company LLC (10 top, 22),
Panini SpA (11 middle).

Cover image: Ted S. Warren/Associated Press

Designer: Ron Jaffe
Series Editor: Mike Kennedy
Content Consultants: Michael Jacobsen and Jonathan Wentworth-Ping
Project Management: Black Book Partners, LLC
Editorial Production: Lisa Walsh

Library of Congress Cataloging-in-Publication Data
Names: Stewart, Mark, 1960 July 7- author.
Title: Seattle Sounders / by Mark Stewart.
Description: Chicago Illinois : Norwood House Press, 2017. | Series: First
    touch soccer | Includes bibliographical references and index.
    Identifiers: LCCN 2016058989 (print) | LCCN 2017014917 (ebook) | ISBN
    9781684040889 (eBook) | ISBN 9781599538693 (library edition : alk. paper)
Subjects: LCSH: Seattle Sounders FC (Soccer team)--History--Juvenile
    literature.
Classification: LCC GV943.6.S43 (ebook) | LCC GV943.6.S43 S84 2017 (print) |
    DDC 796.334/6309797772--dc23
LC record available at https://lccn.loc.gov/2016058989

This publication is intended for educational purposes and is not affiliated with any team, league, or association
including: Seattle Sounders FC, Major League Soccer, CONCACAF, or the Federation Internationale de Football
Association (FIFA).

302N--072017
Manufactured in the United States of America in North Mankato, Minnesota.

CONTENTS

Words in **bold type** are defined on page 24.

Nelson Valdez (#16) is congratulated by teammates Obafemi Martins and Clint Dempsey after his goal in the 2015 playoffs.

MEET THE SOUNDERS

Long ago, the people who measured the depth of the water were called "sounders." The soccer team in Seattle, Washington, is the Seattle Sounders Football Club. In most parts of the world, when people say "football" they are talking about the game of soccer, not American football. The Sounders have the loudest and most loyal fans in the United States. This gives the players extra energy whenever they take the field.

TIME MACHINE

Pro soccer has a long history in Seattle. Fans rooted for a team called the Sounders back in the 1970s. In 2009, the Sounders joined Major League Soccer (MLS). The club began winning right away and never stopped. The Sounders won America's oldest soccer trophy, the U.S. Open Cup, four times in their first six seasons. Their great players include **Eddie Johnson**, Brad Evans, Osvaldo Alonso, and Fredy Montero.

SOUNDERS FC

EDDIE JOHNSON

Fredy Montero gets ready to blast a shot against Vancouver during a 2012 match.

The club's stadium is specially curved so that the sound of cheering fans is as loud as possible.

BEST SEAT IN THE HOUSE

The Sounders play in a stadium built for the Seattle Seahawks football team. The same person, Paul Allen, owns both teams. At first, only 12,000 seats were open for soccer games. Over the years, that number has grown many times. Now the Sounders sell more than 60,000 tickets for important matches.

COLLECTOR'S CORNER

These collectibles show some of the best Sounders players ever.

KASEY KELLER

Goalkeeper
2009–2011
Keller finished his long career with Seattle. He did not allow a goal in his first four games with the club.

CHAD MARSHALL

Defender
First Year with Club: 2014
Marshall played 10 years in MLS before joining the Sounders. He was the league's top defender in 2014.

OBAFEMI MARTINS

Forward

2013–2015

Martins was a great scorer for the Sounders. Seattle fans loved his goal celebrations almost as much as his goals.

CLINT DEMPSEY

Forward

First Year with Club: 2013

Dempsey was a star in England before returning to the U.S. to play for the Sounders. He has scored more than 50 goals for **Team USA**.

CLINT DEMPSEY

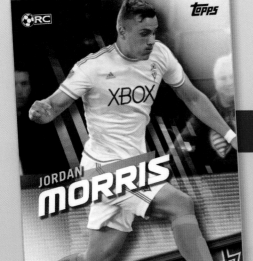

JORDAN MORRIS

Forward

First Year with Club: 2016

Morris grew up in Seattle rooting for the Sounders. He helped them win the **MLS Cup** in his first year with the club.

WORTHY OPPONENTS

The Sounders have a rivalry with the Vancouver Whitecaps and Portland Timbers. They are the two other MLS teams in the Pacific Northwest. These clubs were competing long before they joined the league. All three teams were part of the United Soccer League for many years. The club with the best record against the other two wins the Cascadia Cup. The trophy was the idea of their fans.

Osvaldo Alonso of the Sounders battles for position with a Timbers defender during a 2016 match in Portland.

CLUB WAYS

Half the fun of going to Sounders games is the March to the Match. Before each home game, the fans get behind a marching band called the Sound Wave. It has more than 50 musicians. They march together from Seattle's arts neighborhood to the field. Some say the March to the Match is the greatest tradition in American soccer.

Seattle fans show their passion during the March to the Match before a 2016 playoff game.

ON THE MAP

The Sounders bring together players from many countries. These are some of the best:

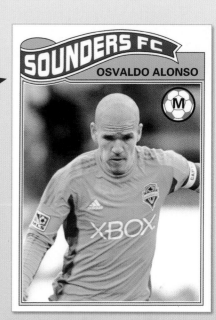

1 **Leonardo Gonzalez** • San Jose, Costa Rica

2 **Osvaldo Alonso** • San Cristobal, Cuba

3 **Will Bruin** • St. Louis, Missouri

4 **Clint Dempsey** • Nagodoches, Texas

5 **Fredy Montero** • Campo de la Cruz, Colombia

6 **Nicolas Lodeiro** • Paysandu, Uruguay

7 **Stefan Frei** • Altstatten, Switzerland

8 **Steve Zakuani** • Kinshasa, Democratic Republic of the Congo

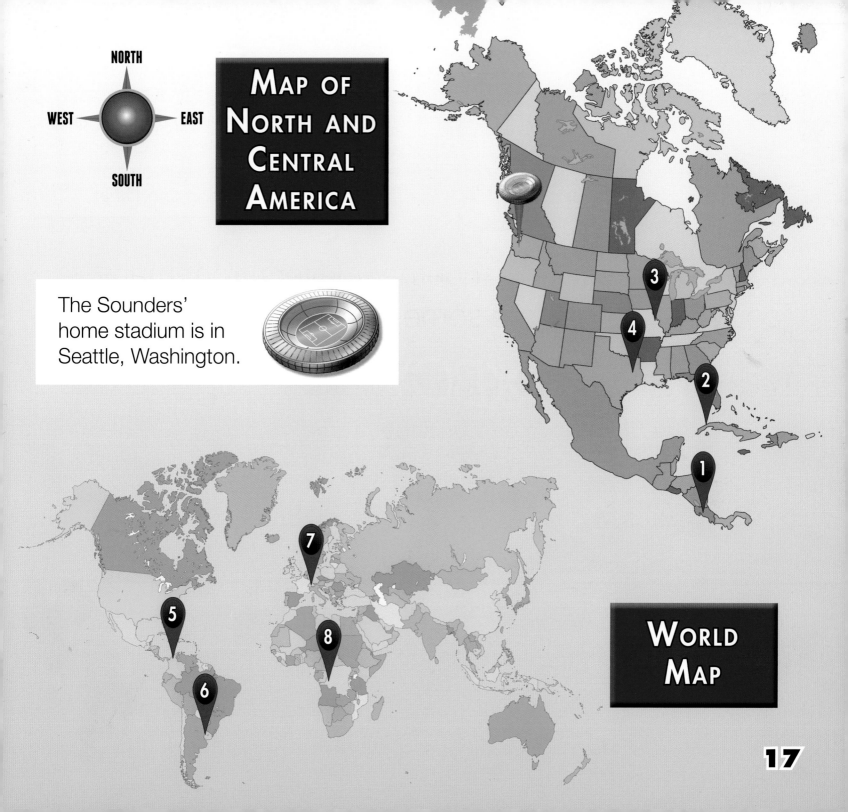

NORTH

WEST ———— EAST

SOUTH

MAP OF NORTH AND CENTRAL AMERICA

The Sounders' home stadium is in Seattle, Washington.

WORLD MAP

Clint Dempsey wears Seattle's home kit during a 2016 game. The club crest can be seen on both his shorts and shirt.

KIT AND CREST

The Sounders wear green from head to toe for home matches. The uniform also has touches of blue. Green stands for the nearby forests. Blue stands for the water. The team's away kit is white, with green and blue stripes. The club's crest is a shield that shows the Space Needle. The Space Needle is the most famous building in Seattle.

WE WON!

The Sounders had an amazing season in 2016. After the worst start in team history, Seattle switched coaches and began winning. They made the playoffs on the final day of the season. The Sounders reached the MLS Cup against Toronto F.C. They did not take one shot on goal during the game, but goalkeeper Stefan Frei did not let Toronto score. The championship was decided in a thrilling **shootout**. Roman Torres made the winning kick.

Roman Torres celebrates Seattle's MLS Cup victory moments after making the winning kick.

21

FOR THE RECORD

The Sounders have won many trophies and titles since joining MLS in 2009!

MLS Cup

2016

U.S. Open Cup

2009

2010

2011

2014

Supporters' Shield*

2014

Cascadia Cup

2011

2015

Freddie Ljungberg

22

The Supporters' Shield is awarded to the MLS club with the best record.

These stars have won major MLS awards while playing for the Sounders:

2009	Freddie Ljungberg • Best XI Midfielder
2011	Kasey Keller • Best XI Goalkeeper
2011	Kasey Keller • Goalkeeper of the Year
2012	Osvaldo Alonso • Best XI Midfielder
2012	Eddie Johnson • Comeback Player of the Year
2012	Patrick Ianni • Goal of the Year
2014	Chad Marshall • Best XI Defender
2014	Chad Marshall • Defender of the Year
2014	Obafemi Martins • Best XI Forward
2014	Obafemi Martins • Goal of the Year
2016	Jordan Morris • Rookie of the Year
2016	Stefan Frei • MLS Cup MVP

Soccer Words

MLS Cup
The championship game of Major League Soccer.

Shootout
A tie-breaker used mostly in championship soccer matches. Each club gets five penalty kicks, with the team scoring the most awarded the victory.

Team USA
The national soccer team that competes against teams from other countries in tournaments like the World Cup.

Index

Photos are on **BOLD** numbered pages.

About the Author

Mark Stewart has been writing about world soccer since the 1990s, including *Soccer: A History of the World's Most Popular Game*. In 2005, he co-authored Major League Soccer's 10-year anniversary book.

About the Seattle Sounders

Learn more at these websites:
www.soundersfc.com
www.MLSsoccer.com
www.teamspiritextras.com